My Family ROOTS

A HISTORY OF OUR FAMILY

POPLAR BOOKS

My Family Roots

Originated by
Julie Hausner
Designed by Stanley Park

Copyright © 1977 Poplar Books Inc.,
a division of Book Sales, Inc.
110 Enterprise Avenue
Secaucus, New Jersey 07094

ISBN 0-89009-133-1   Library of Congress Card No. 77-78952

PICTURE CREDITS: BETTMANN ARCHIVE AND DOVER PUBLICATION; Handbook of Early Advertising Art.

My Family Roots

This Book is Lovingly Dedicated To:

_____

This Record was compiled by:

_____

and started on_____

A family record is more than names, dates and places. It is about people—what they did, the why and the how. This book is designed so you can record forever, in one volume, the history of your family and your ancestors.

There are sections where you can enter the origins of your family: where your ancestors came from and when, what happened to them, and the things they did. You will also be able to record, perhaps for the first time, stories about members of your family that have been handed down from preceding generations. There are other sections devoted to family photographs, traditions and such memorable events as weddings and reunions. And there is a most important "how to" section that will help

you trace your family's history: where to write to obtain records, what information to include in such inquiries, and what institutions are available to you for further assistance (such as libraries and bookstores that specialize in genealogy information).

From the birth of a great, great grandparent to the birth of the newest baby in your family, this book provides a wonderful opportunity to gather together in one place all the interesting and unusual aspects of your family's history. When complete, it will be a storehouse of treasured information, achievements and memories—a permanent record of your family which is unique and not like any other.

CONTENTS

My Genealogy

My Full Name _____

_____

Birth Date _____

Birth Place _____

Father's Full Name _____

Mother's Full Name _____

Brothers and Sisters _____

_____

_____

My Parents

This Certifies that

_____

And

_____

Were United in Holy Matrimony

Place of Ceremony _____

City _____ State _____

Month _____ Day _____ Year _____

Married by _____

_____

Family Tree

MY FULL NAME

DATE OF BIRTH

PLACE OF BIRTH

OCCUPATION

SPECIAL INTERESTS

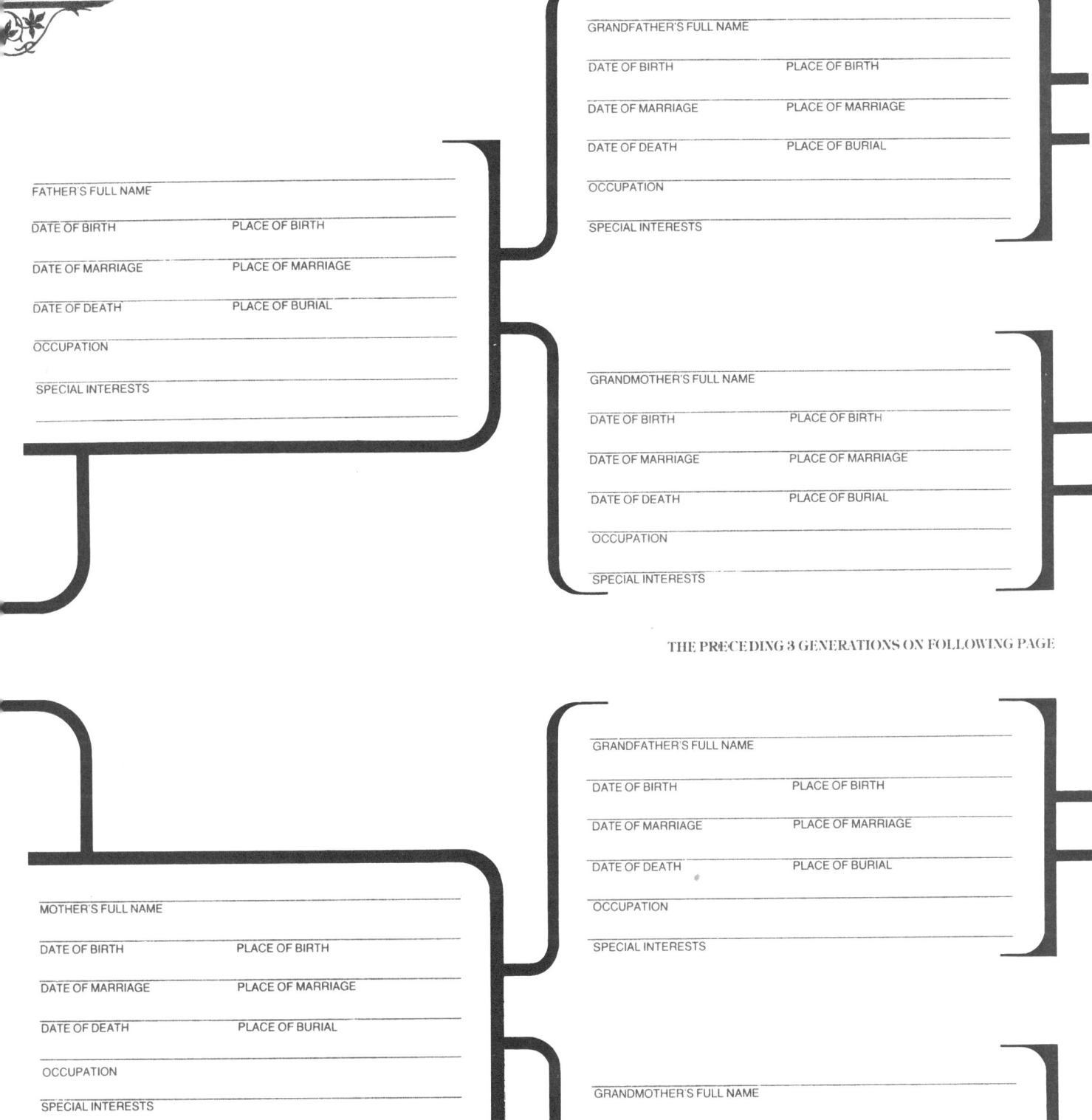

GRANDFATHER'S FULL NAME

DATE OF BIRTH PLACE OF BIRTH

DATE OF MARRIAGE PLACE OF MARRIAGE

DATE OF DEATH PLACE OF BURIAL

OCCUPATION

SPECIAL INTERESTS

FATHER'S FULL NAME

DATE OF BIRTH PLACE OF BIRTH

DATE OF MARRIAGE PLACE OF MARRIAGE

DATE OF DEATH PLACE OF BURIAL

OCCUPATION

SPECIAL INTERESTS

GRANDMOTHER'S FULL NAME

DATE OF BIRTH PLACE OF BIRTH

DATE OF MARRIAGE PLACE OF MARRIAGE

DATE OF DEATH PLACE OF BURIAL

OCCUPATION

SPECIAL INTERESTS

THE PRECEDING 3 GENERATIONS ON FOLLOWING PAGE

GRANDFATHER'S FULL NAME

DATE OF BIRTH PLACE OF BIRTH

DATE OF MARRIAGE PLACE OF MARRIAGE

DATE OF DEATH PLACE OF BURIAL

OCCUPATION

SPECIAL INTERESTS

MOTHER'S FULL NAME

DATE OF BIRTH PLACE OF BIRTH

DATE OF MARRIAGE PLACE OF MARRIAGE

DATE OF DEATH PLACE OF BURIAL

OCCUPATION

SPECIAL INTERESTS

GRANDMOTHER'S FULL NAME

DATE OF BIRTH PLACE OF BIRTH

DATE OF MARRIAGE PLACE OF MARRIAGE

DATE OF DEATH PLACE OF BURIAL

OCCUPATION

SPECIAL INTERESTS

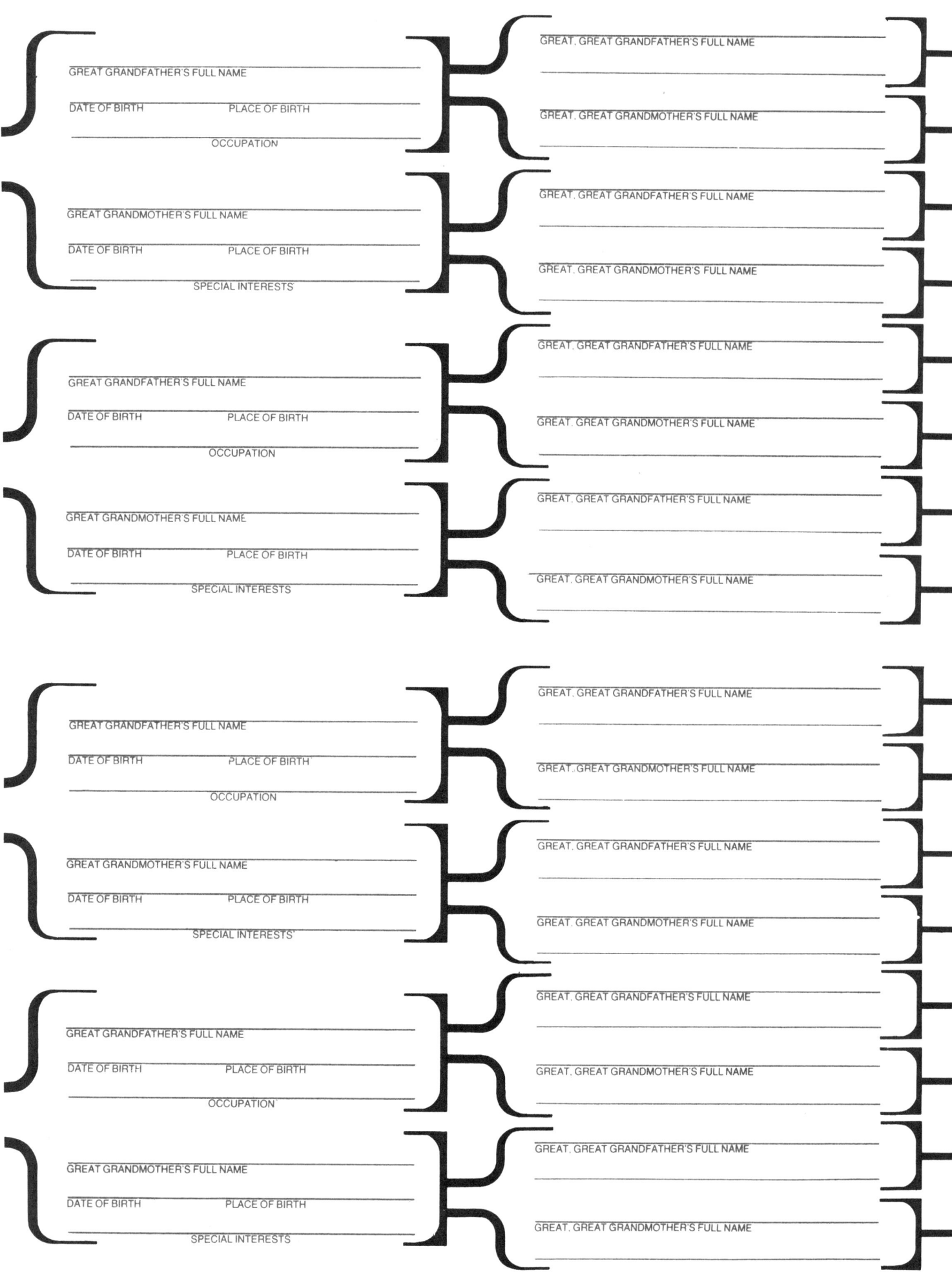

GREAT GRANDFATHER'S FULL NAME

DATE OF BIRTH   PLACE OF BIRTH

OCCUPATION

GREAT GRANDMOTHER'S FULL NAME

DATE OF BIRTH   PLACE OF BIRTH

SPECIAL INTERESTS

GREAT GRANDFATHER'S FULL NAME

DATE OF BIRTH   PLACE OF BIRTH

OCCUPATION

GREAT GRANDMOTHER'S FULL NAME

DATE OF BIRTH   PLACE OF BIRTH

SPECIAL INTERESTS

GREAT GRANDFATHER'S FULL NAME

DATE OF BIRTH   PLACE OF BIRTH

OCCUPATION

GREAT GRANDMOTHER'S FULL NAME

DATE OF BIRTH   PLACE OF BIRTH

SPECIAL INTERESTS

GREAT GRANDFATHER'S FULL NAME

DATE OF BIRTH   PLACE OF BIRTH

OCCUPATION

GREAT GRANDMOTHER'S FULL NAME

DATE OF BIRTH   PLACE OF BIRTH

SPECIAL INTERESTS

GREAT, GREAT GRANDFATHER'S FULL NAME

GREAT, GREAT GRANDMOTHER'S FULL NAME

GREAT, GREAT GRANDFATHER'S FULL NAME

GREAT, GREAT GRANDMOTHER'S FULL NAME

GREAT, GREAT GRANDFATHER'S FULL NAME

GREAT, GREAT GRANDMOTHER'S FULL NAME

GREAT, GREAT GRANDFATHER'S FULL NAME

GREAT, GREAT GRANDMOTHER'S FULL NAME

GREAT, GREAT GRANDFATHER'S FULL NAME

GREAT, GREAT GRANDMOTHER'S FULL NAME

GREAT, GREAT GRANDFATHER'S FULL NAME

GREAT, GREAT GRANDMOTHER'S FULL NAME

GREAT, GREAT GRANDFATHER'S FULL NAME

GREAT, GREAT GRANDMOTHER'S FULL NAME

GREAT, GREAT GRANDFATHER'S FULL NAME

GREAT, GREAT GRANDMOTHER'S FULL NAME

Great, Great, Great Grandparents

MR. & MRS. _____ NEE _____
MR. & MRS. _____ NEE _____

MR. & MRS. _____ NEE _____
MR. & MRS. _____ NEE _____

MR. & MRS. _____ NEE _____
MR. & MRS. _____ NEE _____

MR. & MRS. _____ NEE _____
MR. & MRS. _____ NEE _____

MR. & MRS. _____ NEE _____
MR. & MRS. _____ NEE _____

MR. & MRS. _____ NEE _____
MR. & MRS. _____ NEE _____

MR. & MRS. _____ NEE _____
MR. & MRS. _____ NEE _____

MR. & MRS. _____ NEE _____
MR. & MRS. _____ NEE _____

MR. & MRS. _____ NEE _____
MR. & MRS. _____ NEE _____

MR. & MRS. _____ NEE _____
MR. & MRS. _____ NEE _____

MR. & MRS. _____ NEE _____
MR. & MRS. _____ NEE _____

MR. & MRS. _____ NEE _____
MR. & MRS. _____ NEE _____

MR. & MRS. _____ NEE _____
MR. & MRS. _____ NEE _____

MR. & MRS. _____ NEE _____
MR. & MRS. _____ NEE _____

MR. & MRS. _____ NEE _____
MR. & MRS. _____ NEE _____

The generations preceding the one in the column on the left would have been born about 1800 and of course would be double the number.

Each generation going back in time will be twice the number. If your ancestors landed here in 1600 and you are under 30, you would be the 14th or 15th generation and be descended from over 16,000 people.

For a variety of reasons, families have altered the spelling of the last name or changed it completely. So in looking back and trying to get information from the county, city or town overseas that your family came from, make sure you include as much data as you can get before writing abroad.

NEE REPRESENTS WIFE'S MAIDEN NAME

My Family

On this and the next page, fill in all vital statistics on your brothers and sisters and their children (nieces and nephews).

My Brothers and Sisters and their Children

	BORN	DIED	SPOUSE
Children			
Children			
Children			
Children			
Children			
Children			
Children			
Children			
Children			

Legal Guardians

Parents' Family

On this and the following pages, fill in all vital statistics on your parents, their brothers and sisters (aunts and uncles) and their children (cousins).

Father,
his Brothers and Sisters,
and their Children

	BORN	DIED	SPOUSE
Children			
Children			
Children			
Children			
Children			
Children			
Children			
Children			
Children			

Legal Guardians

(FILL IN NAMES OF LEGAL GUARDIANS FOR ANY CHILD WHERE APPLICABLE. INCLUDING DATES. PLACES AND ANY INFORMATION YOU CONSIDER APPROPRIATE.)

Parents' Family CONTINUED

**Mother,
her Brothers and Sisters,
and their Children**

	BORN	DIED	SPOUSE
Children			
Children			
Children			
Children			
Children			
Children			
Children			
Children			
Children			

Legal Guardians

15

Grandparents—
Father's Side

**Grandfather,
his Brothers and Sisters,
and their Children**

	BORN	DIED	SPOUSE
Children			
Children			
Children			
Children			
Children			
Children			
Children			
Children			
Children			

Legal Guardians

Grandparents—Father's Side

CONTINUED

**Grandmother,
her Brothers and Sisters,
and their Children**

	BORN	DIED	SPOUSE
Children			
Children			
Children			
Children			
Children			
Children			
Children			
Children			
Children			

Legal Guardians

(FILL IN NAMES OF LEGAL GUARDIANS FOR ANY CHILD WHERE APPLICABLE. INCLUDING DATES. PLACES AND ANY INFORMATION YOU CONSIDER APPROPRIATE.)

Grandparents— Mother's Side

Grandfather, his Brothers and Sisters, and their Children

	BORN	DIED	SPOUSE
Children			
Children			
Children			
Children			
Children			
Children			
Children			
Children			
Children			

Legal Guardians

Grandparents— Mother's Side

CONTINUED

Grandmother, her Brothers and Sisters, and their Children

	BORN	DIED	SPOUSE
Children			
Children			
Children			
Children			
Children			
Children			
Children			
Children			
Children			
Children			

Legal Guardians
(FILL IN NAMES OF LEGAL GUARDIANS FOR ANY CHILD WHERE APPLICABLE. INCLUDING DATES. PLACES AND ANY INFORMATION YOU CONSIDER APPROPRIATE.)

Great Grandparents

NAME	BORN	DIED	SPOUSE
Children			
Children			
Children			
Children			
Children			
Children			
Children			
Children			
Children			

Legal Guardians

(FILL IN NAMES OF LEGAL GUARDIANS FOR ANY CHILD WHERE APPLICABLE. INCLUDING DATES. PLACES AND ANY INFORMATION YOU CONSIDER APPROPRIATE.)

NAME	EMIGRATED FROM	TO	DATE

Citizenship Record

In the space below fill in the countries your family came from along with any other information about that place you have or can get. Also put in when the family emigrated, where they landed and how your branch settled where it is now.

NAME	EMIGRATED FROM	TO	DATE

Citizenship Record

Weddings

_____
_____
_____
_____
_____
_____
_____

NAMES	DATE	PLACE

NAMES	DATE	PLACE

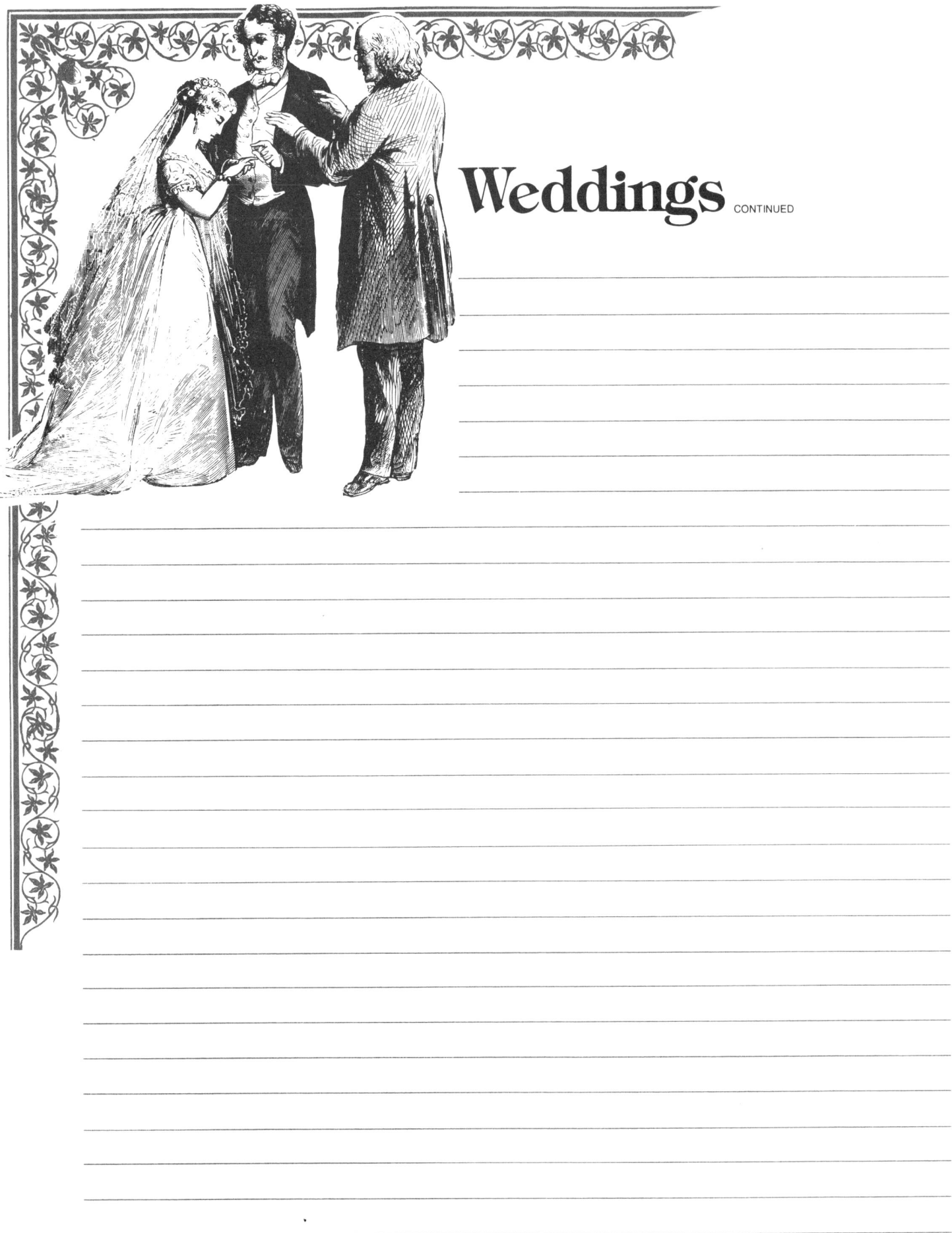

Weddings CONTINUED

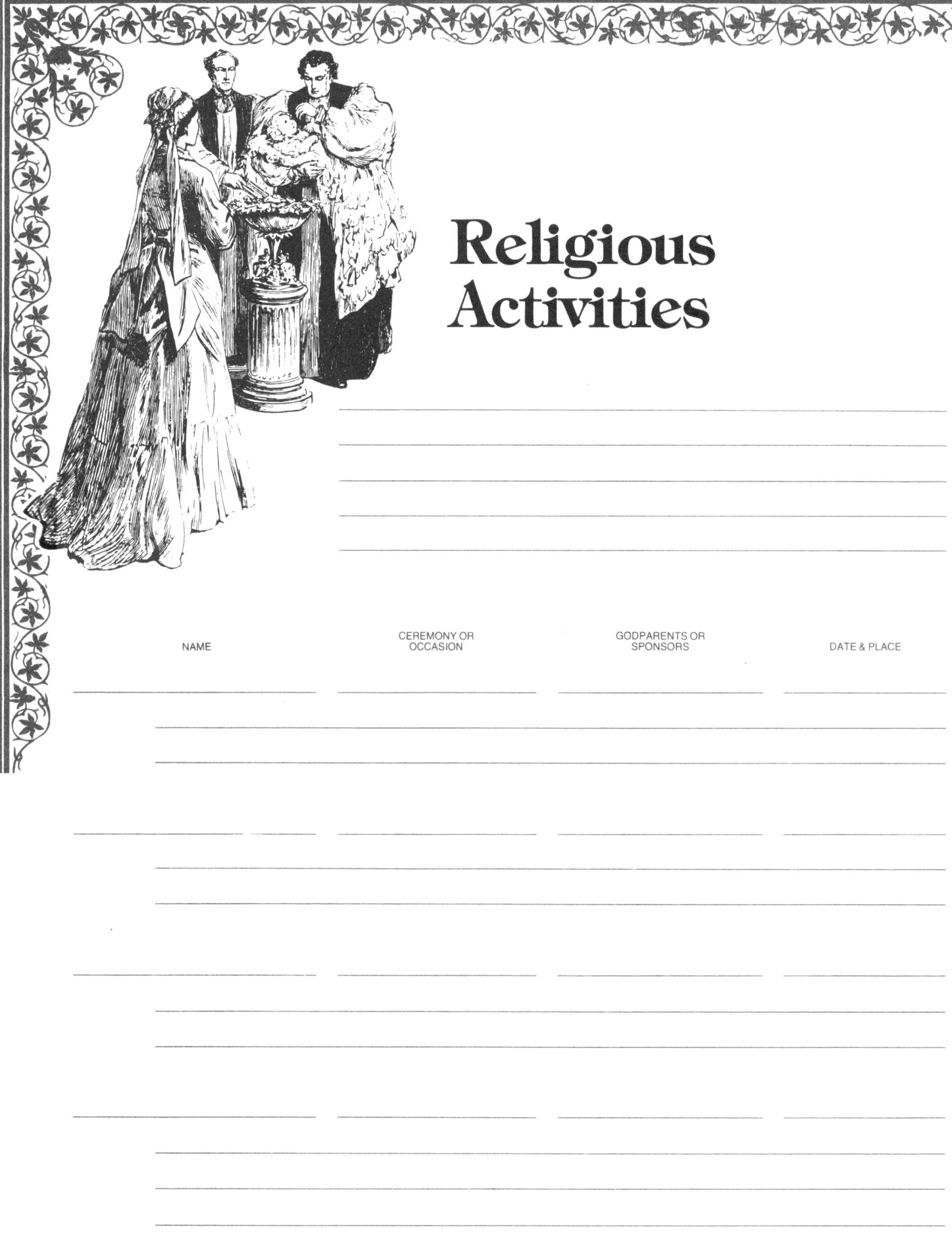

Religious Activities

NAME	CEREMONY OR OCCASION	GODPARENTS OR SPONSORS	DATE & PLACE

NAME	CEREMONY OR OCCASION	GODPARENTS OR SPONSORS	DATE & PLACE

Religious Activities CONTINUED

Our Places of Worship

In Memoriam

Here you may record names of those who have died about whom you have special memories. You may write stories you have heard or your own personal thoughts.

In Memoriam

CONTINUED

Our Homes

Street Address _____

City _____ State _____

Date of Purchase _____ Resided from _____ to _____

_____
_____
_____
_____
_____
_____
_____
_____

Street Address _____

City _____ State _____

Date of Purchase _____ Resided from _____ to _____

_____
_____
_____
_____
_____
_____
_____

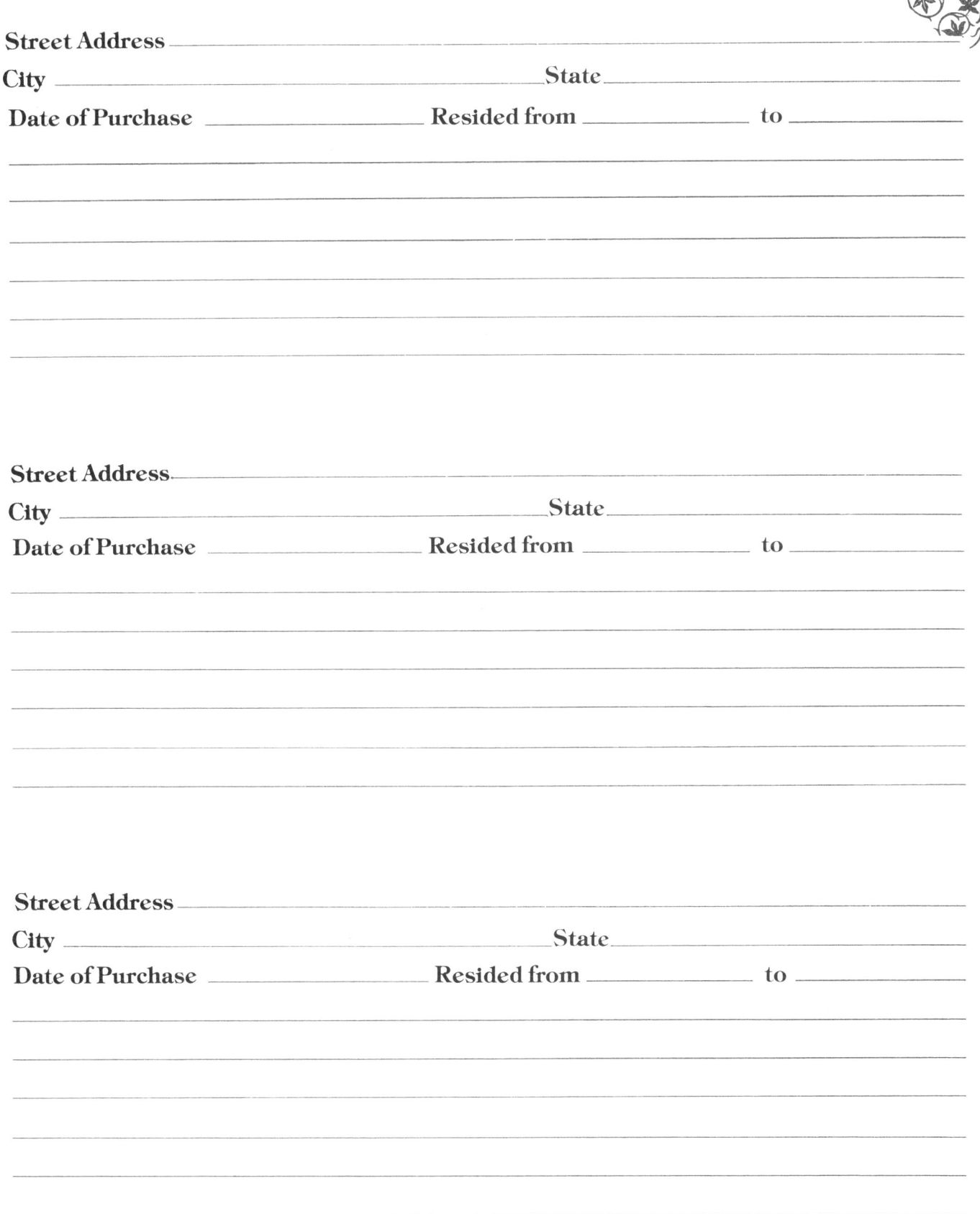

Street Address _____

City _____ **State** _____

Date of Purchase _____ **Resided from** _____ **to** _____

_____

_____

_____

_____

_____

_____

Street Address _____

City _____ **State** _____

Date of Purchase _____ **Resided from** _____ **to** _____

_____

_____

_____

_____

_____

_____

Street Address _____

City _____ **State** _____

Date of Purchase _____ **Resided from** _____ **to** _____

_____

_____

_____

_____

_____

_____

Street Address _____

City _____ **State** _____

Date of Purchase _____ **Resided from** _____ **to** _____

_____

_____

_____

_____

_____

_____

Street Address _____

City _____ **State** _____

Date of Purchase _____ **Resided from** _____ **to** _____

_____

_____

_____

_____

_____

Street Address _____

City _____ **State** _____

Date of Purchase _____ **Resided from** _____ **to** _____

_____

_____

_____

_____

_____

Where My Ancestors Have Lived

Schools

NAME	SCHOOL, COLLEGE OR UNIVERSITY	DATES OF ATTENDANCE	CERTIFICATE OR DEGREE

and Graduations

Schools and Graduations CONTINUED

Important School Achievements—Fine Arts, Athletics and Others

NAME	ACHIEVEMENT	DATE	SCHOOL

Clubs and Organizations

NAME	ORGANIZATION	ACTIVITY, AWARD, OFFICE HELD	DATE

Fill in names of family members and their clubs and organizations, including offices held and any other interesting information about the person or the organization.

Clubs and
Organizations CONTINUED

Companies We Have Worked For or Owned

You may record here employment histories and businesses started by any member of your family, including when and where a business was begun, and its success or failure and why.

Companies We Have Worked For or Owned

CONTINUED

Social Security Numbers

Military Service Records

NAME

SERVICE NUMBER :

JOB CLASSIFICATION :

ENLISTED OR INDUCTED:

MONTH: DAY: YEAR: AT   AGE

BRANCH OF SERVICE   GRADE

TRAINING CAMPS   SERVICE SCHOOLS ATTENDED:

DIVISION: REGIMENT: DEPARTMENT OR SHIP: DATES

COMPANY: TRANSFERRED:

PROMOTIONS AND DATES:

OVERSEAS SERVICE: DEPARTURE DATE   PORT: RETURN DATE   PORT:

BATTLES, ENGAGEMENTS, SKIRMISHES, EXPEDITIONS: COMMANDING OFFICERS: CITATIONS:

WOUNDS RECEIVED IN SERVICE; SICKNESS OR HOSPITALIZATION:

IMPORTANT LEAVES OR FURLOUGHS:

DISCHARGED AT OR SEPARATION.

NAME _____ SERVICE NUMBER: _____ JOB CLASSIFICATION: _____

ENLISTED OR INDUCTED: _____ MONTH: _____ DAY: _____ YEAR: _____ AT   AGE _____

BRANCH OF SERVICE _____ GRADE _____

TRAINING CAMPS _____ SERVICE SCHOOLS ATTENDED: _____

_____

_____

_____

DIVISION: _____ REGIMENT: _____ DEPARTMENT OR SHIP: _____ DATES _____

COMPANY: _____ TRANSFERRED: _____

_____

PROMOTIONS AND DATES: _____

_____

_____

_____

OVERSEAS SERVICE: _____ DEPARTURE DATE _____ PORT: _____ RETURN DATE _____ PORT: _____

_____

_____

_____

_____

BATTLES, ENGAGEMENTS, SKIRMISHES, EXPEDITIONS: _____ COMMANDING OFFICERS: _____ CITATIONS: _____

_____

_____

_____

_____

WOUNDS RECEIVED IN SERVICE; SICKNESS OR HOSPITALIZATION: _____

_____

_____

IMPORTANT LEAVES OR FURLOUGHS: _____

_____

DISCHARGED AT OR SEPARATION. _____

Military Service Records CONTINUED

NAME

SERVICE NUMBER:

JOB CLASSIFICATION:

ENLISTED OR INDUCTED:

MONTH: DAY: YEAR: AT AGE

BRANCH OF SERVICE GRADE

TRAINING CAMPS SERVICE SCHOOLS ATTENDED:

DIVISION: REGIMENT: DEPARTMENT OR SHIP: DATES

COMPANY: TRANSFERRED:

PROMOTIONS AND DATES:

OVERSEAS SERVICE: DEPARTURE DATE PORT: RETURN DATE PORT:

BATTLES, ENGAGEMENTS, SKIRMISHES, EXPEDITIONS: COMMANDING OFFICERS: CITATIONS:

WOUNDS RECEIVED IN SERVICE; SICKNESS OR HOSPITALIZATION:

IMPORTANT LEAVES OR FURLOUGHS:

DISCHARGED AT OR SEPARATION.

NAME _____ SERVICE NUMBER: _____ JOB CLASSIFICATION: _____

ENLISTED OR INDUCTED: _____ MONTH: _____ DAY: _____ YEAR: _____ AT   AGE _____

BRANCH OF SERVICE _____ GRADE _____

TRAINING CAMPS _____ SERVICE SCHOOLS ATTENDED: _____

_____

_____

_____

DIVISION: _____ REGIMENT: _____ DEPARTMENT OR SHIP: _____ DATES _____

COMPANY: _____ TRANSFERRED: _____

_____

PROMOTIONS AND DATES: _____

_____

_____

_____

OVERSEAS SERVICE: _____ DEPARTURE DATE ____ PORT: _____ RETURN DATE ____ PORT: _____

_____

_____

_____

_____

BATTLES, ENGAGEMENTS, SKIRMISHES, EXPEDITIONS: _____ COMMANDING OFFICERS: _____ CITATIONS: _____

_____

_____

_____

WOUNDS RECEIVED IN SERVICE; SICKNESS OR HOSPITALIZATION: _____

_____

_____

IMPORTANT LEAVES OR FURLOUGHS: _____

_____

DISCHARGED AT OR SEPARATION. _____

Military Service Records CONTINUED

NAME _____

SERVICE NUMBER : _____

JOB CLASSIFICATION : _____

ENLISTED OR INDUCTED: _____

MONTH: _____ DAY: _____ YEAR: _____ AT AGE _____

BRANCH OF SERVICE _____ GRADE _____

TRAINING CAMPS _____ SERVICE SCHOOLS ATTENDED: _____

_____

_____

DIVISION: _____ REGIMENT: _____ DEPARTMENT OR SHIP: _____ DATES _____

COMPANY: _____ TRANSFERRED: _____

PROMOTIONS AND DATES: _____

_____

_____

OVERSEAS SERVICE: _____ DEPARTURE DATE _____ PORT: _____ RETURN DATE _____ PORT: _____

_____

_____

BATTLES, ENGAGEMENTS, SKIRMISHES, EXPEDITIONS: _____ COMMANDING OFFICERS: _____ CITATIONS: _____

_____

_____

WOUNDS RECEIVED IN SERVICE; SICKNESS OR HOSPITALIZATION: _____

_____

IMPORTANT LEAVES OR FURLOUGHS: _____

DISCHARGED AT OR SEPARATION. _____

NAME _____ SERVICE NUMBER: _____ JOB CLASSIFICATION: _____

ENLISTED OR INDUCTED: _____ MONTH: _____ DAY: _____ YEAR: _____ AT AGE _____

BRANCH OF SERVICE _____ GRADE _____

TRAINING CAMPS _____ SERVICE SCHOOLS ATTENDED: _____

_____

_____

_____

DIVISION: _____ REGIMENT: _____ DEPARTMENT OR SHIP: _____ DATES _____

COMPANY: _____ TRANSFERRED: _____

_____

PROMOTIONS AND DATES: _____

_____

_____

_____

OVERSEAS SERVICE: _____ DEPARTURE DATE _____ PORT: _____ RETURN DATE _____ PORT: _____

_____

_____

_____

_____

BATTLES, ENGAGEMENTS, SKIRMISHES, EXPEDITIONS: _____ COMMANDING OFFICERS: _____ CITATIONS: _____

_____

_____

_____

_____

WOUNDS RECEIVED IN SERVICE; SICKNESS OR HOSPITALIZATION: _____

_____

_____

IMPORTANT LEAVES OR FURLOUGHS: _____

_____

DISCHARGED AT OR SEPARATION. _____

Military Service Records CONTINUED

NAME

SERVICE NUMBER:

JOB CLASSIFICATION:

ENLISTED OR INDUCTED:

MONTH: DAY: YEAR: AT AGE

BRANCH OF SERVICE GRADE

TRAINING CAMPS SERVICE SCHOOLS ATTENDED:

DIVISION: REGIMENT: DEPARTMENT OR SHIP: DATES

COMPANY: TRANSFERRED:

PROMOTIONS AND DATES:

OVERSEAS SERVICE: DEPARTURE DATE PORT: RETURN DATE PORT:

BATTLES, ENGAGEMENTS, SKIRMISHES, EXPEDITIONS: COMMANDING OFFICERS: CITATIONS:

WOUNDS RECEIVED IN SERVICE; SICKNESS OR HOSPITALIZATION:

IMPORTANT LEAVES OR FURLOUGHS:

DISCHARGED AT OR SEPARATION.

NAME _____ SERVICE NUMBER: _____ JOB CLASSIFICATION: _____

ENLISTED OR INDUCTED: _____ MONTH: _____ DAY: _____ YEAR: _____ AT AGE _____

BRANCH OF SERVICE _____ GRADE _____

TRAINING CAMPS _____ SERVICE SCHOOLS ATTENDED: _____

_____

_____

_____

DIVISION: _____ REGIMENT: _____ DEPARTMENT OR SHIP: _____ DATES _____

COMPANY: _____ TRANSFERRED: _____

_____

PROMOTIONS AND DATES: _____

_____

_____

_____

OVERSEAS SERVICE: _____ DEPARTURE DATE _____ PORT: _____ RETURN DATE _____ PORT: _____

_____

_____

_____

_____

BATTLES, ENGAGEMENTS, SKIRMISHES, EXPEDITIONS: _____ COMMANDING OFFICERS: _____ CITATIONS: _____

_____

_____

_____

_____

WOUNDS RECEIVED IN SERVICE; SICKNESS OR HOSPITALIZATION: _____

_____

_____

IMPORTANT LEAVES OR FURLOUGHS: _____

_____

DISCHARGED AT OR SEPARATION. _____

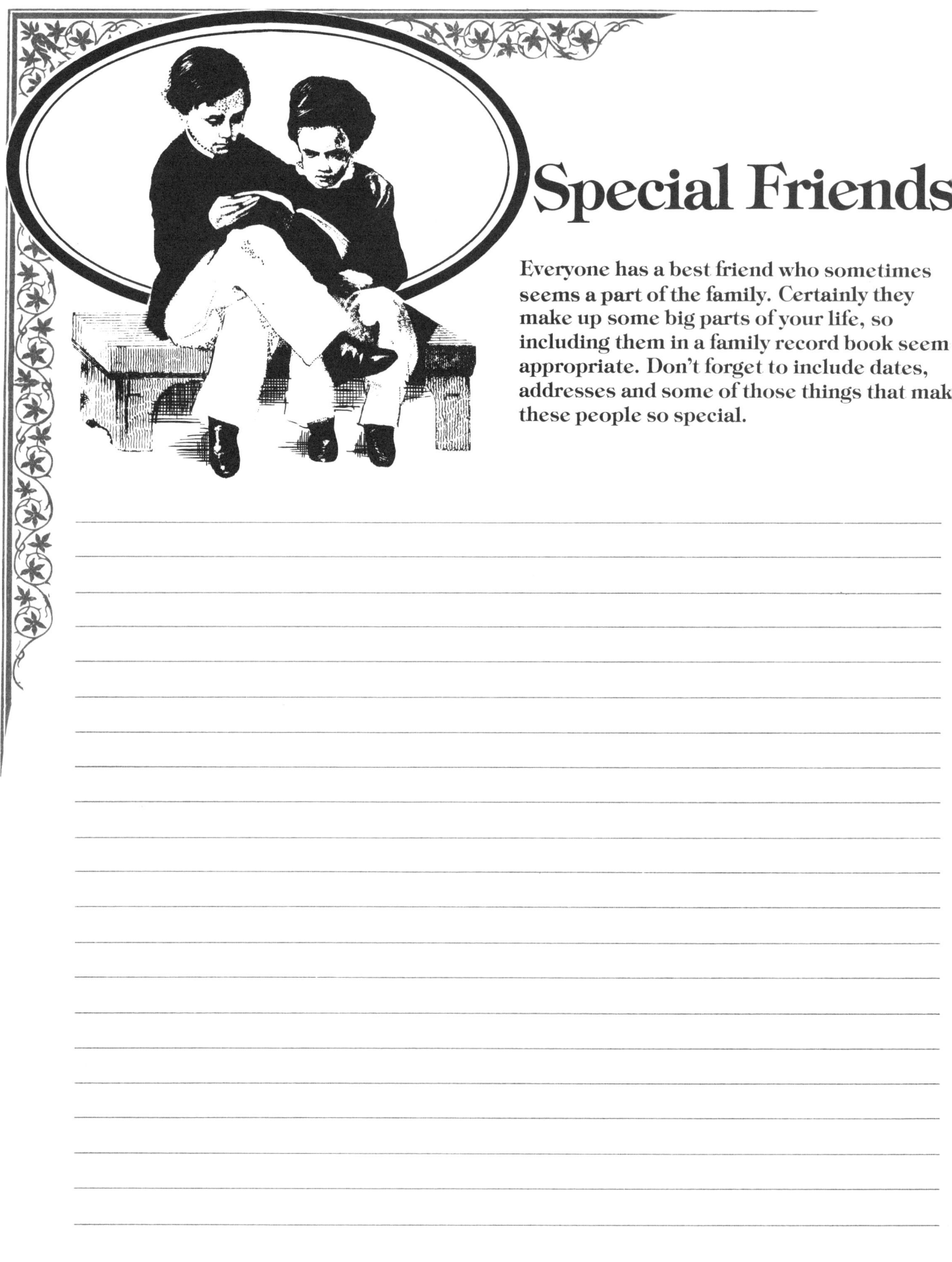

Special Friends

Everyone has a best friend who sometimes seems a part of the family. Certainly they make up some big parts of your life, so including them in a family record book seem appropriate. Don't forget to include dates, addresses and some of those things that mak these people so special.

Special Friends

CONTINUED

Our Pets

The chances are millions to one that you have a pet elephant but more than likely you have a dog, cat, turtle or fish. Animals, like good friends, seem to become part of the family and play a part in our daily lives. Because they are integrated into the 'family,' remembering them will recall fond memories.

OWNER	PET'S NAME	TYPE OF PET	DATES OF OWNERSHIP

Family
Automobiles

OWNER	MAKE, MODEL, YEAR	COLOR	DATES OF OWNERSHIP

Americans have always been a people on the move and ever since Henry Ford started to mass produce cars they have been a part of almost every family's life. Every auto you have owned or will own has a special place in your life and remembering them will bring back lots of memories.

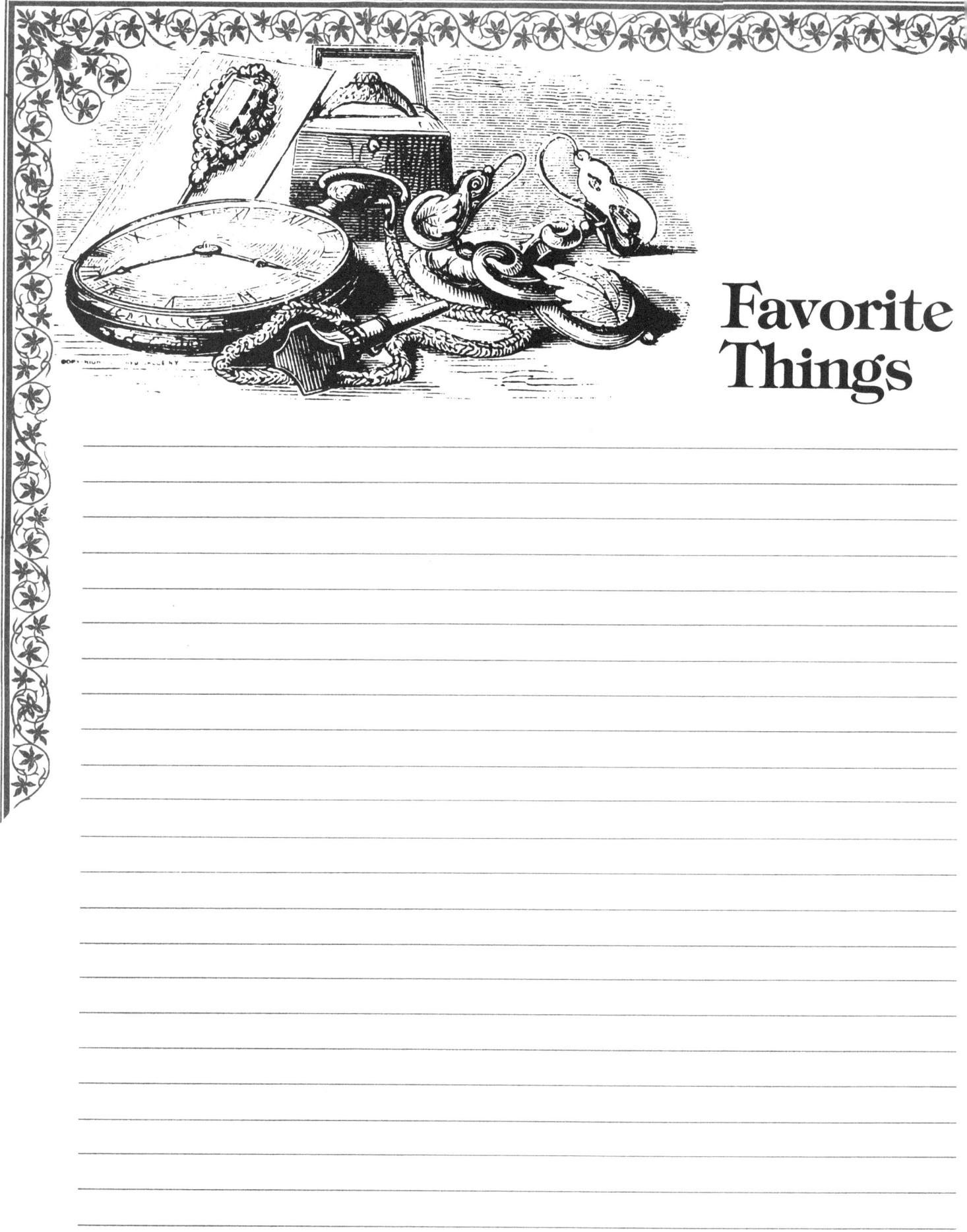

Favorite Things

Songs—Records
Books—Shows
Places—Recipes, etc.

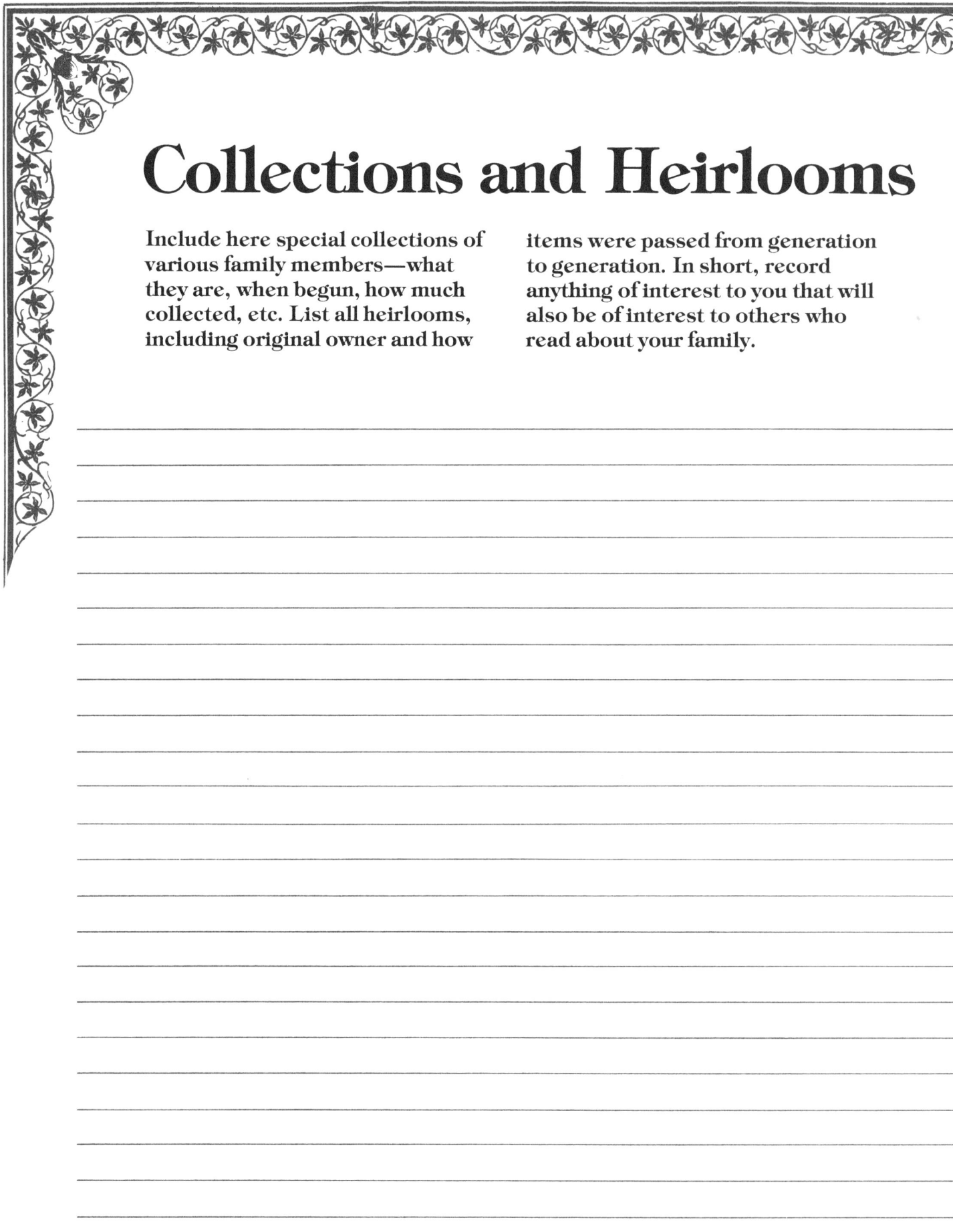

Collections and Heirlooms

Include here special collections of various family members—what they are, when begun, how much collected, etc. List all heirlooms, including original owner and how items were passed from generation to generation. In short, record anything of interest to you that will also be of interest to others who read about your family.

Collections and Heirlooms

CONTINUED

Favorite Family Sports

FAMILY OR INDIVIDUAL'S NAME	SPORT, TEAM, CLUB	SPECIAL ACHIEVEMENT

Favorite Family Sports CONTINUED

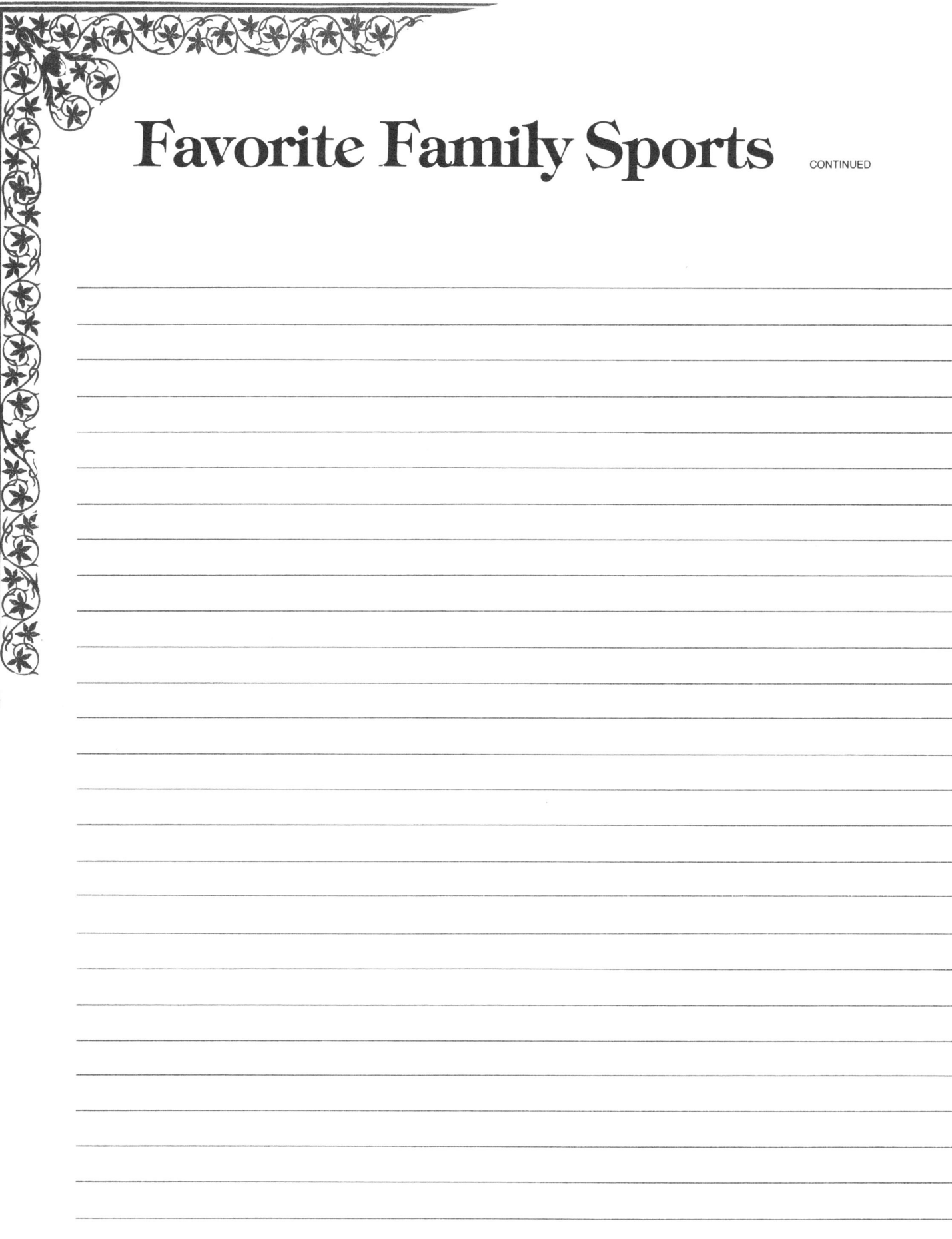

Favorite Family Hobbies

From woodcarving and quilt making to rebuilding old cars and raising exotic plants, many families have individuals who pursue a wide variety of interesting hobbies. Here is space to record those individuals and their pastimes and any fascinating pieces of information about how they started and why and whether anyone else followed in their footsteps.

Favorite Family Hobbies

CONTINUED

Family Vacations

Getting away from it all seems to keep us going through the rest of the year so entering some of the places you go to, who was there, and what happened can help bring back some of that fun. Some vacations are not so much where you went as what you did or who you met, so by recording this you have the chance, in the future, to look back and smile or cry.

Family Vacations CONTINUED

Family Reunions

Remembering who was there and at what occasion is a lot easier if you record it here. In years to come this kind of information will conjure up the event all over again for you. No matter whether it was your fifth high school class reunion or the family's Fiftieth Wedding Anniversary.

who was there

Family Reunions CONTINUED

Family Traditions

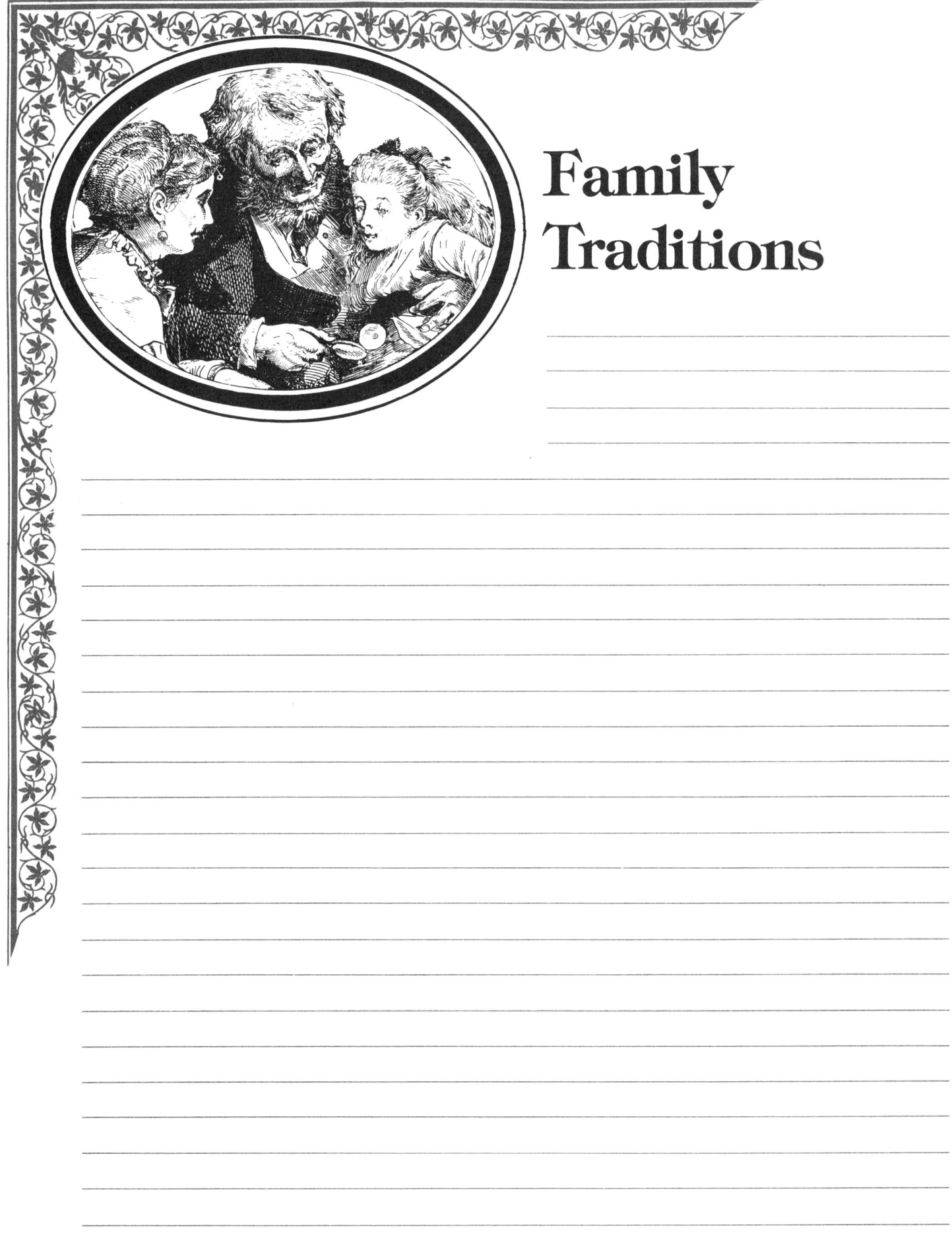

Family Traditions

Events to Remember

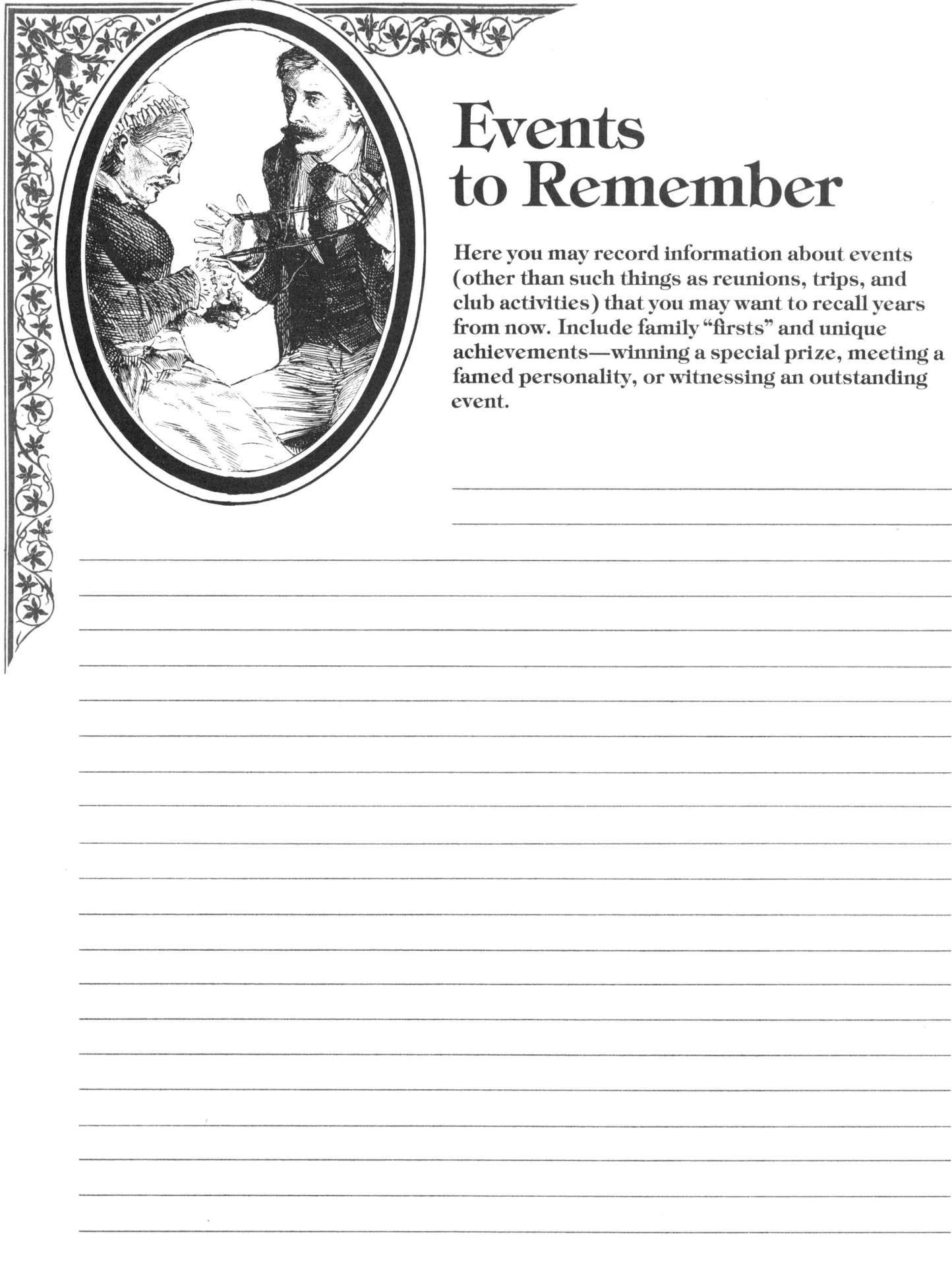

Here you may record information about events (other than such things as reunions, trips, and club activities) that you may want to recall years from now. Include family "firsts" and unique achievements—winning a special prize, meeting a famed personality, or witnessing an outstanding event.

Events to Remember CONTINUED

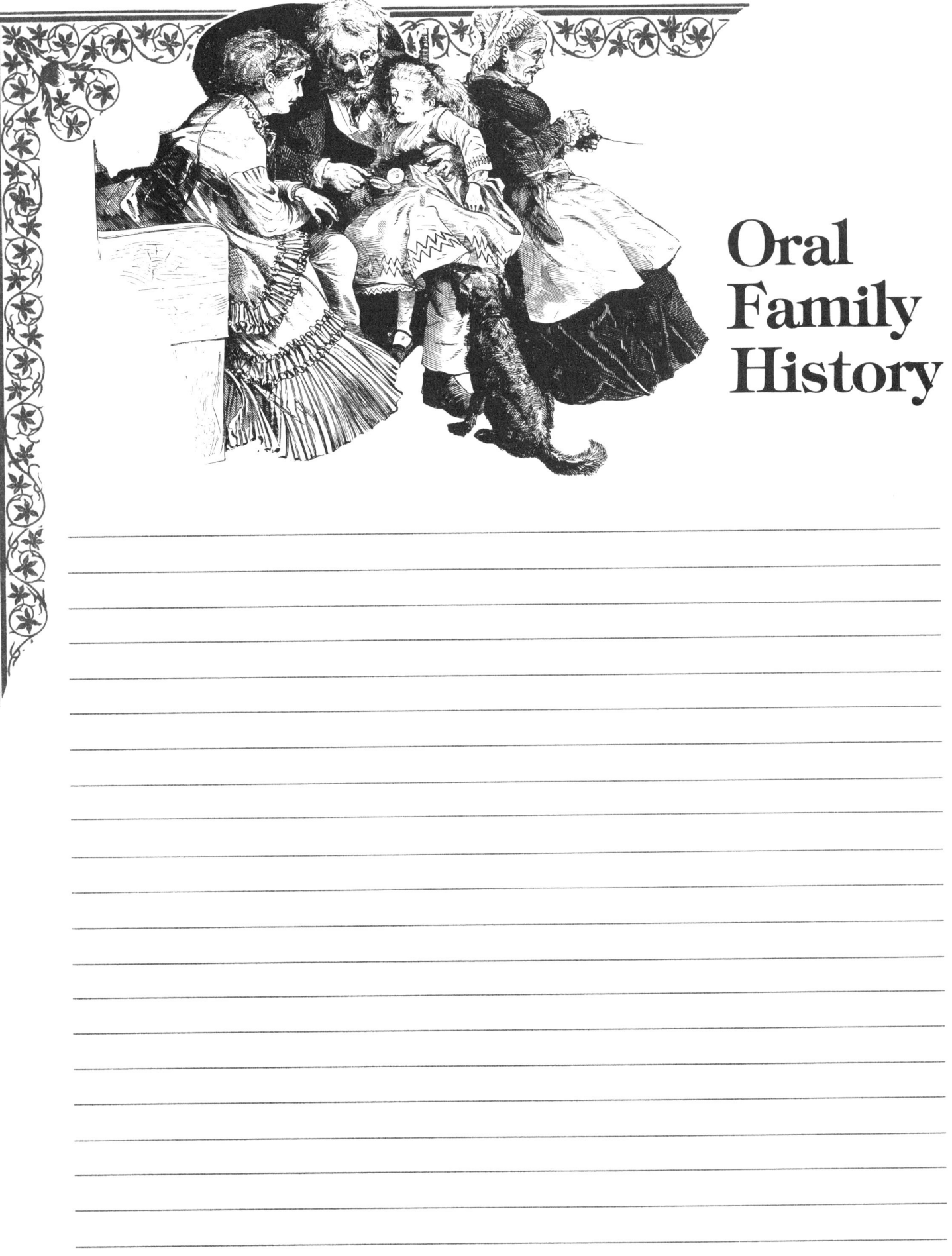

Oral Family History

From survivors and participants in wars to migrations from other countries, each family has stories no one has ever written down. Here is space to do so to record forever what will be lost if it remains "oral history."

Oral Family History

CONTINUED

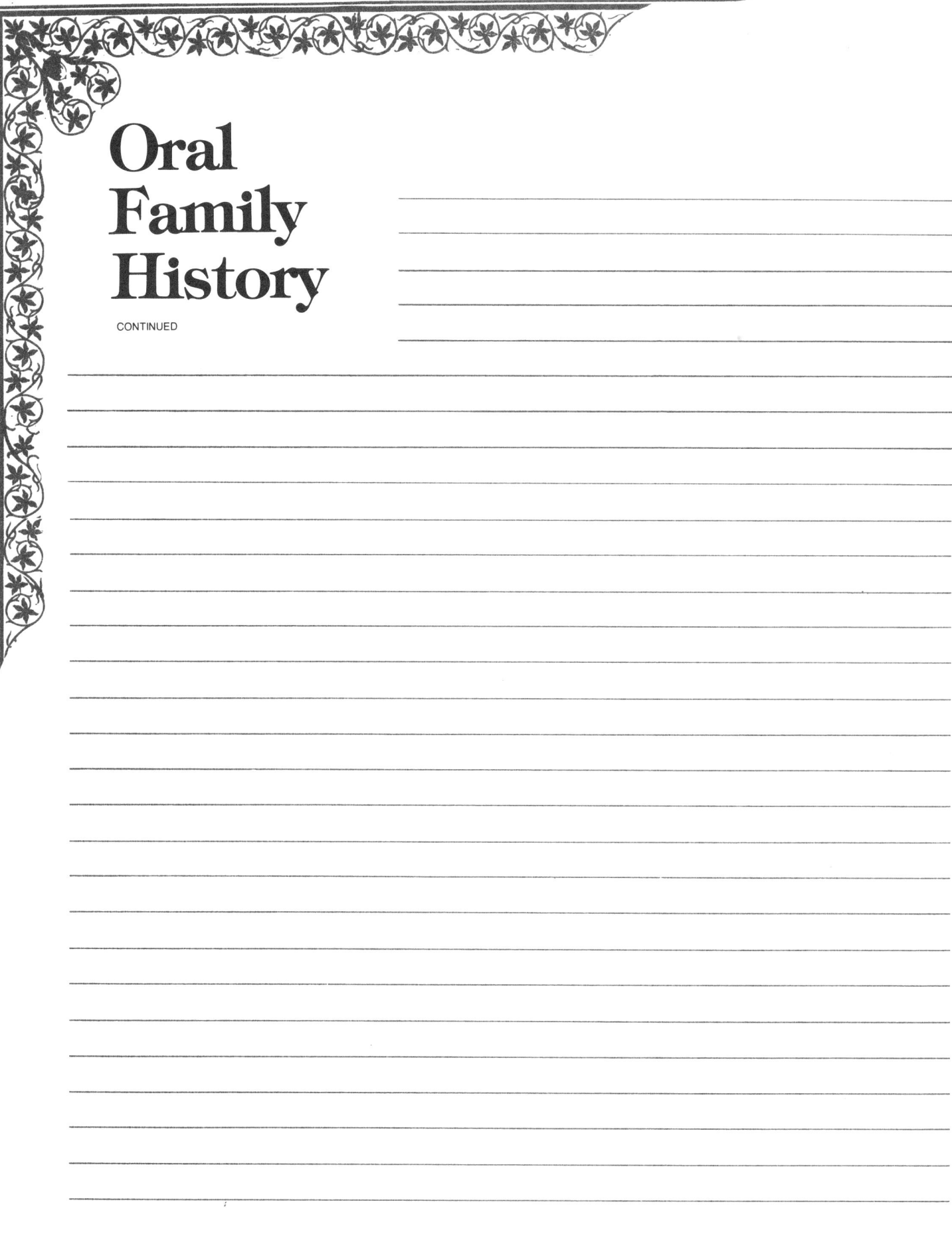

Oral
Family
History CONTINUED

Oral Family History

CONTINUED

Extraordinary Events
We Have Survived and Overcome

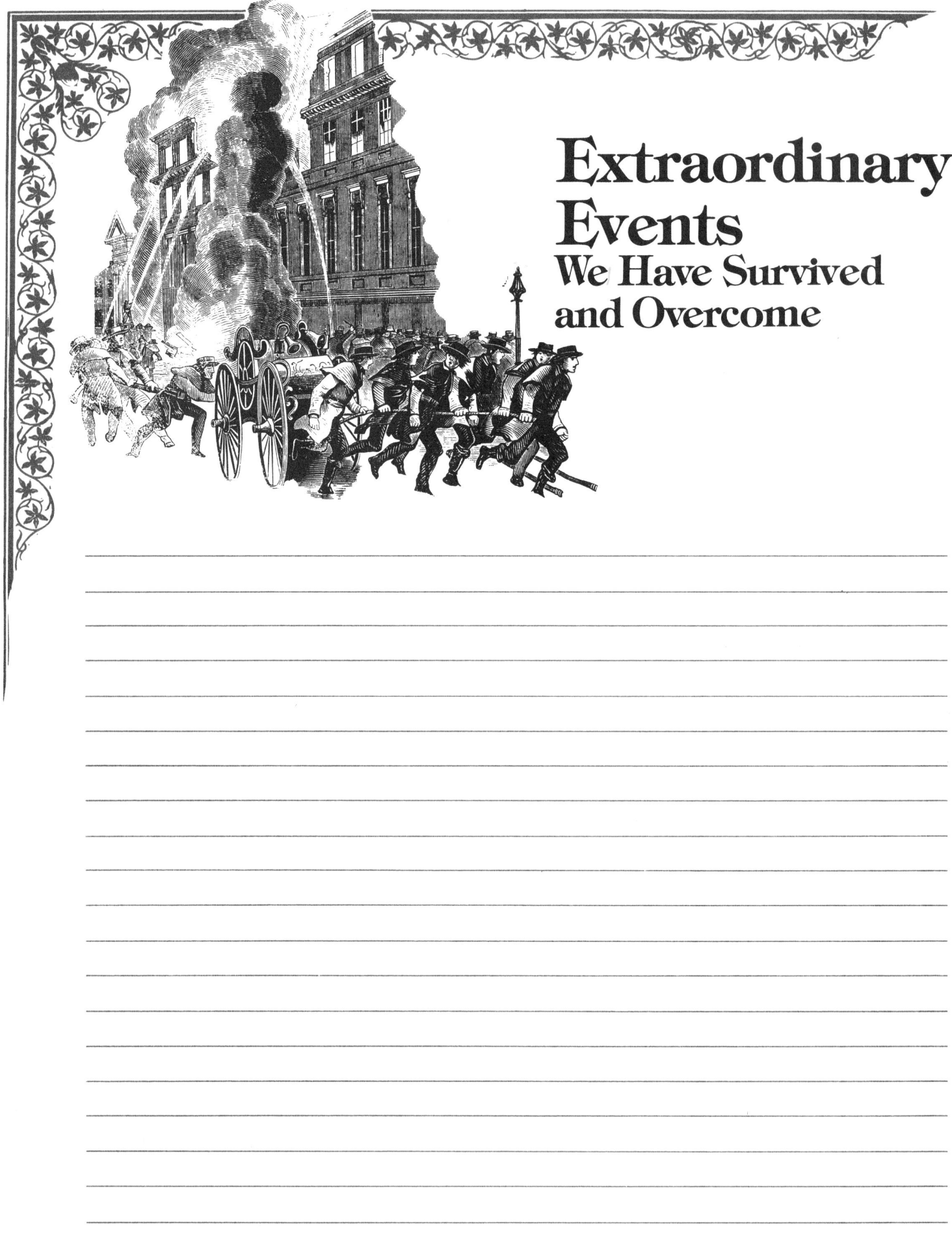

Into each family come those unforeseen events. Many have survived natural disasters (floods, tornados) and many times families were forced to move or lives were altered for the better as a result. Here is space for you to record whatever you feel is appropriate in relation to your own family's experiences.

Illnesses

NAME	ILLNESS. OPERATION	HOSPITAL. DOCTOR	DATE

Vital Statistics

NAME	Height	Weight	Hair Color	Color of Ey

Color Preference

it Size ess Size	Blouse Size Shirt Size	Shoe Size	Hat Size	Ring Size	Other Sizes

Photographs

Pictures do their own story telling and in years to come a lot can be learned from this kind of record. You and future generations will be able to look back and see a member of the family in his or her own time and place. (You may also want to include favorite clippings, mementos, or documents.)

Photographs

CONTINUED

Photographs

CONTINUED

Genealogy Research

All of us know something about our living relatives. We enjoy telling stories about their achievements and exploits, and we certainly have a fondness for the endearing characters which are in most families. Yet our knowledge of our families often does not go beyond those members we actually know. Few of us have been lucky enough to have known our greatgrandparents for example. This shows us that one of the most common ways of learning about ourselves is by word of mouth; the so-called oral tradition. Thus, if you want to begin finding out more about your family the place to start is with your relatives. Ask them if they can provide you with the birth dates, places of residence and dates of death of those who you do not know, such as your greatgrandparents. Do this as far as it is possible to trace them. Once you have reached this point you will often discover the great treasures of information available in family bibles, picture albums, old letters, diaries and account books. Your ancestors often kept better records than you think!

Once you have names, dates and places you can consult town records. Securing birth certificates, marriage licenses, death certificates, wills and land deeds will give you additional names you will want and need. Don't be disappointed if some of these public records are not available. You can always check your public library. Some of the subjects you can look up at the library are clans, deeds, epitaphs, estates, marriage licenses, nobility, parish registers, peerage and precedence. Also don't forget to ask the librarian for additional sources of genealogical information. If the books listed in the card catalogue should not be in the stacks, your librarian can easily send for them.

Another place to check is your state genealogical association or historical society. Each state has its own organization with qualified people who can be very helpful in local matters. These associations also often publish their own periodicals which you might like to look into. The Daughters of the American Revolution in your area may also be able to furnish you with further information. Sometimes they too publish interesting pamphlets on the subject.

The next step in your search is to contact the National Archives, which is the central United States depository for records, located in Washington, D.C., to find out which of their eleven regional branches is nearest to you. The Archives contain many different kinds of records which will be helpful to you. The Census Records, from 1790 to date, are kept here. They give information such as the name of each member of a family, his age, occupation and place of birth. Also available are records of military service, pensions and land grants. Since we are a nation of immigrants you may find here the names of the first members of your family who came to America, as well as the name of the ship that brought them, the date of arrival, the port of entry and the date of naturalization. For other such information one should consult the United States Immigration and Naturalization office.

Some helpful hints and dos and don'ts in tracing and checking your family record.

For the majority of us our families have only lived in America for three or four generations. It was about this time that the mass immigration from other countries to the United States began. Thus far, all of the research information has concentrated on relatives who lived in America. There is no need to stop searching at this point however, because there are sources available to help you trace your ancestors to the countries that they originally came from. The library of the Church of Jesus Christ of Latter-Day Saints in Salt Lake City contains the largest collection of genealogical information dating from 1538 to 1805. It contains records from the National and local archives, courthouses, cemeteries, churches and a variety of other places where records were kept, about people all over the world. Some 40 countries are represented in this collection of genealogical data. This enormous library has branches around the world and since they require that you do your own research you can write to them to find out which of the twenty branches is closest to you. The library's researchers are continually making copies of genealogical records throughout the world to further expand the collection.

For the most part at this point you have completed all of the research that can be done in America and it is time to write away to foreign countries to get additional information. To find out where and to whom to write you should contact the consulate of the country to which you are writing. The telephone book will provide you with its address in Washington, D.C. Once the consulate has sent you the correct address and the name of the person to whom you should write, do not hesitate because you don't speak the language; the agency will get someone to translate your letter for them. It is very important to include as much pertinent information as you have. Names, dates, places of residence are especially necessary. One thing you must consider is that often when people arrived in America from other countries their names were misspelled or arbitrarily anglicized and therefore you must know what their name was originally before you make any inquiries.

Do not get discouraged, as you can see there are many sources to help you to find information. To give you an idea of what results your search for your roots can lead to, let us take an historical example. It has been 350 years since the arrival of the Mayflower in 1620, which means there have been about 13 generations of your family since that time. These 13 generations represent more than 16,000 direct descendants.

To account for all of these ancestors in order to have a complete genealogical chart would be an imposing task even for an expert, and, if you continued to expand the charts used in this book by the time you reached 1600 that column would have over 8,000 spaces for names and be over 165 feet tall. If you decide after doing some searching on your own that you need the help of a professional researcher, write for a list of qualified genealogists. Some people who did not have a written language will have to rely on the records of others. To say the least, at most times they are inaccurate and distorted. Even the South American Indians, who did have a written language, lost it, so all natives of the Western Hemisphere and Black Africans will have to seek out oral family or tribal histories which many times cannot pinpoint a place, person, or date but in general are quite close to fact. Do not be taken in by the commercially advertised mail-order coat-of-arms trade.

The charts which appear in this book go back five generations, about 150 years. These five generations represent about 124 people in a direct line descendancy.

ADDRESSES TO WRITE TO

Where to write for booklets on how and where to find vital records:

Superintendent of Documents
United States Government Printing Office
Washington, D.C. 20402

The three booklets are:
1. "Where to Write for Birth and Death Records." 1967 (Public Health Service Publication No. 630A, 35¢.)
2. "Where to Write for Marriage Records." 1965. (Public Health Service Publication No. 630B, 35¢.)
3. "Where to Write for Divorce Records." 1965. (Public Health Service Publication No. 630C, 35¢.)

The National Archives and Records Service
General Services Administration
Washington, D.C. 20408

The Church of Jesus Christ of Latterday Saints
50 E. North Temple Street
Salt Lake City, Utah 84150

Board for the Certification of Genealogists
1307 New Hampshire Avenue
N.E. Washington, D.C.

BOOKSTORES WHICH SPECIALIZE IN GENEALOGICAL MATERIAL

Goodspeed's Book Shop
18 Beacon Street
Boston, Mass. 02108

Chas. E. Tuttle
Rutland, Vt. 05701

Genealogical Book Co.
Baltimore, Md. 21202

BIBLIOGRAPHY

American Genealogical Research Institute. **How to Trace Your Family Tree.** Dolphin Books.

Bennett, Archibald F. **Finding Your Forefathers in America.** Salt Lake City, Bookcraft Co., 1957.

Bidlack, Russell Eugene. **First Steps in Climbing the Family Tree.** Detroit Society for Genealogical Research, 1966.

Doane, Gilbert H. **Searching for Your Ancestors.** New York, Bantam Books, Inc., 1974.

Everton, George B. **The Handybook for Genealogists.** Logan, Utah, Everton Publishers, 1962.

Greenwood, Val D. **The Researcher's Guide to American Genealogy.** Genealogical Publishing Co., 1973.

Iredale, David. **Discovering Your Family Tree.** Shire Publications.

National Genealogical Society. Special Publications: No. 17, **Genealogy, Handmaid of History.** (A list can be obtained of other articles on the subject from the Society, 1921 Sunderland Place, N.W., Washington, D.C. 20036.)

Rottenberg, Dan. **Finding our Fathers.** New York, Random House, 1977.

Williams, Ethel W. **Know Your Ancestors.** Rutland, Vt., C. E. Tuttle Co., 1964.